Retirement Rx

Small Doses of Wisdom, Inspiration & Truth

By Robert Laura

ISBN-10: 0-9754250-5-6
ISBN-13: 978-0-9754250-5-3

Published with RetirementProject.org

Table Of Contents

Dedication

None of this would be possible without my relationship with God and the loving support of my wife Amie and our blended family of four children!

Introduction

Traditional retirement plans are often designed to get people from point A to point B. However, as you begin to sketch out this seemingly straightforward journey, it's easy to forget that, like the first explorers, there are sections of every map that are uncharted, with boundaries outside of what can be seen, explained, or anticipated.

It's not uncommon to overlook these voids and simply assume they will remain outside the mapped area. Yet, instead of considering the unknown as off limits or out of the picture, I want to encourage you to embrace and explore them. To walk off the path in order to survey the depths of your heart and soul, seeking out those distant places, and expanding the retirement horizon instead of putting boundaries around it.

Approaching retirement planning as a voyage that embraces both the known and the unknown leads to very different conversations and results. The discussions will be more fun, creative, and personal, and they'll be more meaningful.

Despite the many freedoms that retirement is supposed to offer you, venturing off a traditional planning path isn't part of the playbook for many people. As a result, they can be apprehensive about discussing these new frontiers and putting their thoughts and ideas on paper. People assume if they have the right amount of money and reach a certain age, everything will just work out. They have been medicated to believe that retirement is all about the dollars and cents, and that they'll figure it out when they get there.

But nothing in life comes that easy. Too often, vague or general assumptions about what life in retirement may be like can lead to disappointment, frustration, and learning things the hard way later. Yet, retirement doesn't need to be a strange place where we end up, full of excuses as to why so much of life ended up in the background, out of sight and off the map.

Instead consider this book like a new prescription or vaccine for retirement. Just as a physician injects a small dose of a germ into our body so that we can develop a natural defense against it, retirees must be given a small dose of what it is going to be like to retire in order to defeat unrealistic expectations and reduce reality shock once they get there.

This new retirement treatment requires more than a single dose and must be accompanied by a commitment to invest as much time and energy in yourself as you have with the financial aspects of retirement. It means starting to infuse your life with new steps and actions—because great personal stories and family legacies aren't created by following the same plan as everyone else. Instead, they are blazed by going where there is no path and leaving a trail for others to follow.

On the following pages, you will find small doses of wisdom, inspiration and truth. Don't feel confined to following the normal page order or my editor's preference for guided structure. Meander through the material at your own pace, taking time to stop and enjoy this new lease on life in retirement. Get the most out of your experience by journaling your new discoveries and inspiring others by sharing your findings with us and those around you.

Fishing For The Big Ones

Gary was an avid fisherman and found his way into the bait and tackle aisle of every store he could. During one trip he noticed a young boy about 10 years old standing alone by the lures.

He was pleased to see the young man taking an interest in the more advanced stuff, instead of just assuming that worms and a bobber were the only way to go. So, he struck up a conversation with the young angler by asking, "See anything good over here?"

The young man turned to him with a somewhat serious look and replied, "Not really, the purple worms and a frog work best for me."

That's when Gary caught a glimpse of the giant frog lure the kid had in his hands. It not only covered his entire palm but looked big enough to be showcased at a county fair.

The sheer size of the frog and the boy's sincere answer caught Gary off guard, causing him to laugh aloud and say, "Wow, that's a pretty big frog isn't it?"

Gary wasn't trying to be condescending or to make the young kid feel like he was out of his league and should change his selection, but it just seemed so ridiculous to Gary.

That's why Gary was surprised when the boy turned to him and without hesitation said, "Not if you're trying to catch the big ones!"

The kid tipped his ball cap at Gary and left him standing in the aisle dumbfounded, but with a valuable lesson: Don't be afraid to go for the big one, no matter what other, more experienced people think!

In other words, don't let mainstream ideas or perceptions about retirement dictate what you should do in this next phase of life. Go big and don't be afraid to challenge the status quo. It's an invigorating attitude to carry in life.

Reflections:

What aspects of your retirement life and plan are you going for the big one with? What do you feel lured to accomplish in retirement?

How have you gone against the grain in the past or challenged the status quo?

What pre-conceived notions or limitations have you had to rise above?

A Bittersweet Transition

Larry is a respected financial planner who is occasionally called upon to serve as an expert financial witness in divorce cases—primarily, when one spouse tries to hide assets in order to avoid splitting them.

In one case, Larry was called into the court room and asked to take the stand. In most court proceedings, the attorney who hired him has to prove that he's an authority in his field of expertise. Therefore, he has to read off all of Larry's impressive credentials, experience, and career accolades.

As the attorney meandered through the disclosures, Larry sat on the right hand side of the judge patiently waiting to testify when out of the blue, the defendant (ex-husband) broke court protocol. He blurted out, "Okay, there is no way I know as much as this financial guy and, yes, there was money in the account that I did not include during the divorce proceedings."

The judge immediately called the attorney and ex-husband to the bench. The judge advised they adjourn the proceeding and that the two men should meet in the hallway to reach a settlement, which they did.

Larry was dismissed and as he walked out of the courtroom, the attorney and defendant graciously thanked him. Larry smiled and was glad to be part of the winning team but the entire situation ended up being bittersweet. On the one hand, he didn't have to say a word—no testimony, cross examination, or submission of court exhibits. Nothing.

On the other hand, he had spent hours preparing for that moment, including hours of reviewing relevant forms and statements, researching historical prices for a variety of stocks, and then summarizing it all into several documents. He was paid handsomely for all his time and effort, yet the case resolved so unexpectedly, it left him feeling somewhat unfulfilled.

At first, Larry joked with family and friends about how easy it was to make that money. But there was something else he wasn't talking about. He actually wanted to testify. He wanted to share the work he did, how he did it, have the court recognize his expertise, and convey to both plaintiff and defendant his determination to get to the bottom of this situation.

To make matters more confusing, a week before this case was tried, Larry was complaining to his wife about the workload, how it took longer than expected, and that he probably should have turned down the case.

Was Larry happy, mad, or sad? Frankly, he actually felt all of them and was experiencing something called competing feelings. It is very common and shouldn't be dismissed, especially when you get closer and closer to retirement.

As people make their way to and through retirement, they can experience a wide variety of feelings, which sometimes don't seem to make sense. Some retirees may have complained about their job in the past, but miss it when they retire. Others may have plenty of money saved and invested, but miss the buzz of problem solving, or being part of a team environment. And yet, many of these same retirees can find joy in their newfound freedom to wake up without an alarm clock.

In any case, you're not alone in feeling bittersweet about retirement. Which makes it important to avoid glossing over your thoughts and feelings, and spending hours trying to solve emotional problems that may take time to sort out and work through.

Reflections:

What are the different feelings you have had or are having about retirement?

What are the things that excite you and those that concern or worry you?

Write down two people that you can contact for advice about what it takes to adapt to retirement.

The Secret Message In Chaos

Bill and Mary normally sat in the same section of church and rarely missed a service, especially now that Bill was retired. Shortly before mass began, a young mother of two walked in and sat just across from them. As she began to organize her boys and their things, Bill cracked his crooked smile at them. Then he nudged Mary, wondering why the kids were in there.

It was fairly uncommon to see young children in this area because the church had a dynamic and well-staffed area for kids. Additionally, each service was projected onto a large screen just outside the main worship hall for families that needed space for kids to express themselves, but didn't want to use the childcare.

Bill shrugged it off and prepared to listen to the week's message. Then without warning, chaos began to reign down. Both boys had small toy trains that made an annoying winding sound as they pushed them along the seats near them. Being toddlers, they clashed with each other, laughing out loud one moment, crying for help the next. They shoved each other, raced up and down the aisle, dropped their snacks on the floor, and did everything conceivable to make sure those around could not hear or follow the weekly message.

Both Bill and Mary were surprised by the fact that despite all the chaos taking place, the mother wasn't fazed. Not once did she get up or even remotely try to get them to settle down into a church-like manner. Mary and a few other more experienced mothers in the surrounding seats did their best to cope. A few gave the mother a polite gaze suggesting, "Would you mind trying to pull it together over there?"

As if things couldn't get any worse, Mary noticed Bill sigh and try to discretely cover his nose. One of the boys pooped in his pants, and the stench filled the east end of the church. Once again, the mother did nothing. At this point, any reasonable parent would have gathered up their things, apologized, and exited as quickly as possible. Instead, the mom sat there and the kids seemed to ramp up their frenzied behavior.

Bill tried his best to tune out the kids, but he couldn't help feeling distracted by the blatant display of chaos and the mother's inability to manage it. At this point, Bill felt the message was a complete loss because the kid's constant action and noise made the pastor sound like Charlie Brown's teacher, "Wah-wa-wah-wa-wah."

And then it suddenly hit him. The message he was supposed to hear wasn't coming from the pulpit this week. It was coming from the situation taking place right in front of him. The impromptu realization made him grin as he shook his head in disbelief.

You see, what Bill came to understand was that although none of us want to admit it, there are aspects of our lives that are in disarray or causing turmoil. They may not be on full display as this mother's situation was, but they are there. They are very real, and if we don't acknowledge them and begin to work on them, they can create challenges for us and those around us.

Our ability to manage or deal with them has a lot to do with what we can and can't control. As much as Bill and Mary wanted to remedy the church situation, they had no control of this mother and her kids. They had to decide whether to storm out, as a few people did, or they could find a lesson among the mess.

Truth be told, at some point during retirement, we will make annoying sounds, clash with each other, and laugh one moment only to cry for help the next. We'll likely try to shove our ideals onto future generations, maybe unexpectedly drop things that once seemed so important, and God forbid, even struggle to control our bowels.

The reality of life is very much the same for this mother and for people entering retirement. There is no single best way to go about it. Although it's easy to cast judgment and doubt on others, we all experience seasons of life that don't fit into everyone else's sense of order and well-being. Retirement can be a lot to manage and no matter how big or small your challenges are, it's all about finding the right perspective.

Reflections:

Are there some things you're trying to manage that may be out of your control?

Are there fresh lessons to be learned from frustrations you're experiencing?

What message could you be missing that may free you from your current chaos?

Facing Your Fears

David's grandparents had a really cool basement. It had an out-of-tune piano he could pound on, a long closet full of old coats and clothes he could play hide-and-go-seek in, and his grandfather was an electrician who loved to tinker so he had a small workshop filed with wires, switches, and all sorts of gadgets.

He loved everything about it - except one area. Buried deep in one corner was the furnace room. It was a dark and ominous spot that was simply terrifying. A place that made him shiver and shake whenever he looked at it or walked near it. It was in the furthest corner of the basement, had no windows, and despite the lights over the laundry area, it only glowed by the flames within the belly of the furnace.

His grandparents also had a small refrigerator near the furnace room and occasionally would store food and drinks in it before a family get-together. On special occasions, he would be asked to go down and grab a few things from it. Fear would immediately grip him because every time he ventured near it, he felt something dark and daunting hanging over him, anxiously waiting for the Boogie Man to grab him.

Then one hot summer day he ventured down to the basement to cool off and felt compelled to face his fears and enter the furnace room. He fought the urge to turn around, and he grabbed a big yellow flashlight from his grandfather's workshop, took a couple deep breathes to build some courage, and walked-in.

His mind was racing as images of finding the skeleton of a bag lady or colony of giant rats swirled in his head.

But to his surprise he found something he never expected. Instead of a gruesome or frightening discovery, he found a small storage area where his uncle had left his old sports equipment, some trophies, and baseball cards.

For a sports-loving kid this was equivalent to finding a pot of gold under the rainbow. David was fanatical about baseball cards at the time, and he loved the idea of trying on his uncle's old hockey gloves and playing catch with his well-worn baseball mitt.

In an instant the furnace room was transformed from a dark, scary cavern to a gold mine. The basement he thought was great before became even better as a whole new area was open and able to be experienced.

It's an eye-opening story because certain parts of your life and retirement plans may be similar to a furnace room - holding you back and blinding you to the treasures you could be experiencing.

Reality is, fear is human nature, so we all experience it. As we get older, we may not verbalize these feelings as being scared or afraid because we have learned to replace them with words like stress or anxiety, but it doesn't matter. They can all grip us and stop us from living an abundant life, filled with new adventures and knowledge.

Whether you're afraid of being alone, losing a loved one, staying healthy, or running out of money, the longer you wait to open up that furnace room door, the harder it's going to be.

Reflections:

What is your biggest retirement fear that is acting like a furnace room in your life?

How might it be holding you back or blinding you to the treasures you may find after walking through them?

Share a time in your life you had to summon up extra courage to face a fear or major problem in your life. How did you do it?

Changing Your Course

During a naval training exercise riddled with poor weather conditions and heavy fog, a battleship's lookout reported to the captain, "Steady light, bearing on the port bow, sir."

The admiral called out, "Signal that ship! "We are on a collision course! Advise you to change course 20 degrees."

A return signal was quickly received, "Advisable for you to change your course 20 degrees."

Growing impatient, the assertive admiral, called out to the signalman, "Signal: I am a Navy admiral! Change your course 20 degrees now."

Seconds later the signal was returned, "I'm a seaman second class. You had better change your course 20 degrees."

Furious, the admiral shouted, "Send: I am a battleship. Change course 20 degrees immediately."

A final signal was returned, "I am a lighthouse."

The admiral changed his course.

Retirement can often function like a lighthouse in the distant fog. No matter what you have been trained to think about it, or believe, there will be

times you're going to end up like this admiral—
frustrated and maybe even a little embarrassed.
So, the key to a successful retirement is watching
for signals and having a little humility.

Reflections:

*Which aspects of your retirement plan might be on
a collision course?*

*What are the signals that you are seeing that
suggests you may need to change course?*

*What steps can you take to remain humble and
open to other people's advice, even if they are only
a seaman second class?*

The Cunning Thief

Little Bobby walked behind Dad into his house like he always did, but without warning, everything changed.

The first sign something was wrong was that his normally hyperactive dog, was cowering in the corner, instead of jumping all over him. Then he saw wires dangling from the wall where the TV and VCR used to be. The household decorations that helped to make their house a home were all broken, missing, or scattered. Bobby didn't understand what happened.

Their home had been burglarized in broad daylight. For the first time in his young life, he felt a victim's fear and distrust. Up until then, much of his 12-year-old life was about what he could have, what he could do, and what he could be. Now for the first time, he felt forced to worry more about protecting what he had, rather than reaching for more.

In an eerily similar way, retirement can be a cunning and deceptive thief - capable of stealing your most prized possessions from you. Just as being robbed can be a harsh reality for those who are unprepared, walking through the door of retirement can result in the same disheartening feelings. You can become a victim, stunned by the loss of things that once made you feel valuable, structured, and connected to others.

Unfortunately, many of these robberies are overlooked and never get reported to people that can help, as evidenced by eye witness accounts from loved ones dealing with the ramifications of a retirement break-in.

One wife said, "Tim still checks his flight schedule every day. He logs in to see where he would be flying if he were still on the job. He checks the weather, and then all day he stares aimlessly at the TV. I don't know what to do with him."

A concerned daughter shared, "I don't know what my dad does out there in that pole barn during the day, but every morning he wakes up like he's got somewhere to go, heads out there and doesn't come back in until supper time. We've invited him to do other things and encouraged him to get in touch with some work friends or re-connect with some buddies from his old neighborhood, but he doesn't say much and keeps to himself like never before."

I don't know the police code for missing persons, but as you can see from these examples, lost identity is one of the most devastating things retirement can rob from a person. Primarily because people often confuse who they are with what they do, and once the routine, daily schedule, and purpose are altered, they lose a piece of themselves that can take years to redefine and rebuild.

Less severe forms of theft also occur throughout retirement. Although not as extreme as having your home broken into, if something is stolen from your car, garage, or toolbox, you may not immediately feel the need to replace it. However, you may realize later how important that item was in your life.

It's like that in retirement, too. Fading relationships in retirement, especially with former co-workers, may not seem like a major loss at first, but over time, a retiree may come to realize how crucial they are to one's overall well-being. The comfort and ease of work relationships are not easily replaced, and new ones can be hard to find.

Regrettably, people are left to solve many of these retirement robberies on their own. But it doesn't have to be that way. You can walk through the door of retirement with plans to protect your relationships and secure a new identity in retirement with the following reflections.

Reflections:

What aspects of your work life are most likely to be robbed from you in retirement?

Who are you when you are not working? What hobbies, activities, or passions excite you?

What work relationships are the most fruitful, fun, or engaging? How do you plan to maintain them?

Making A Splash

Memorial Day was here and for Rose and her family it marked the start of swimming pool season. As you might expect, her kids couldn't wait for the pool to open. Without fail, each of her four kids constantly asked about the exact day and timing of their first swim—no matter how many times she clarified it for them.

She was amused by the fact that year after year, the kids never remembered what truly awaited them at the opening of swim season. Like most kids, they were so convinced that it was going to be the best thing ever, and the idea of it being extremely cold, never really registered.

Rose, however, knew that the pool would be freezing, but warning the kids felt like a waste of time. That's because they never actually got the message until they were in the pool!

After organizing all the towels, toys, and snacks for the day, Rose and the kids made their way down to the pool. Their excitement reached a fever pitch as they slid open the large glass door. With goggles on, a few favorite toys in hand, and even wearing flippers, they bee-lined for the clear, blue water.

Rose attempted to yell some last minute instructions, "Don't run! And be careful," but those fell on deaf ears as her oldest daughter Ava made a mad dash to be the first one in the pool. Within seconds you heard her splash. She never bothered to test the waters, but just launched in. As soon as her head popped back above the water she exclaimed, "Oh, my gosh, it's freezing! Oh, my gosh! Oh, my gosh!" "It's freezing," she said until she reached the pool ladder.

As if his sister's warnings didn't matter, Rose's youngest son Drake was the second one to take the plunge. Likewise, he didn't test the water and just jumped in. However, unlike his sister, Drake entered the pool with a mission. He had brought his diving mask and had thrown some diving sticks around the pool. Once he was in, he didn't get out. He stayed occupied for almost two hours. Rose eventually referred to him as her little "polar bear" for his ability to block out the chilly temps.

Her other two kids chose very different paths than the first two. Connor and Luke eased their way in by way of the stairs. The eldest child, Connor never really adjusted. The threat of it being cold and not having any toys to play with, left him exiting frequently for the comfort of a towel and sunshine.

Luke on the other hand, took a football which seemed to take his mind off the cold for a while, but also became a source of frustration as the other kids were either busy playing something else or were not in the pool to toss it back and forth.

Overall, it's easy to see how the children entered the pool as a perfect metaphor for the way many people enter retirement. Some just jump in and immediately realize that it's uncomfortable and may not be as much fun as they expected.

Others seem to acclimate better, but they do so because they have a plan for everyday life, and it may include some sort of diving sticks to keep them focused and busy.

Another segment of retirees never really acclimate and may wander aimlessly through it. Meanwhile, others may experience social ups and down based on who is around to play with.

No matter how you choose to enter retirement, it's important to understand that people adapt in different ways based on their perceptions, aspirations, and experience.

Reflections:

How do you plan to enter retirement? Compare and contrast your personal style in taking on new things.

What do you plan to use as your diving sticks to fend off the cold waters of retirement?

What aspects of retirement do you plan to do on your own? Which aspects with others?

Watered-down Relationships

While discussing retirement at a seminar, an advisor raised a glass of water and asked, "How much does this glass of water weigh?"

After fielding some answers, the advisor said, "The weight depends on how long you try to hold it. If you hold it for a minute, that's not a problem. If you hold it for an hour, your arm will ache. If you hold it for a day, you'll have to call an ambulance."

"In each case, it's the same weight, but the longer you hold it, the heavier it becomes. And that's the way it is with relationships in retirement. The longer couples go without discussing their thoughts and plans, and developing a set of shared expectations, the bigger and heavier the issues can become."

"Sooner or later, unmet expectations or differences of opinion will turn into ongoing arguments or long-standing resentments, and you won't be able to hold them. As with the glass of water, you have to put those burdens down in order to achieve the retirement you both deserve."

Before you save another dime towards retirement, take some time to share your thoughts and opinions about retirement. Set some ground rules to help avoid common pitfalls and missteps. Invest in each other by not only discussing but also writing down your individual thoughts, feelings, and expectations.

What does a perfect day together in retirement look like?

What are some things you each plan to do on your own or with others that doesn't include a spouse?

What are the benefits to spending some time together and some time apart?

An Inside-Out Approach

Frank and Diane had just put the kids to bed, and Frank reached out to give his wife a hug. As Diane walked away, a tag on her shirt caught his eye.

Frank cautiously asked, "Honey, is your shirt inside out?"

Without even checking, she exclaimed, "No!"

Frank never claimed to be a fashion expert, and these days you never know if a tag on the outside is some sort of new fad or something, but he persisted, "Well babe, you have this tag hanging out here."

Diane was irritated by Frank's response as she asserted, "I've had this on...."

However, before she could finish her sentence, she had looked down and gasped, "Oh, my gosh! It really is inside out. I can't believe no one told me," she said. Then she rattled off all the places she went, including the grocery store, post office, and library.

"I went to all those places and nobody stopped to tell me."

As she walked back towards the kitchen, the couple laughed about it. After a short pause, Frank asked, "It's so late, are you going to turn it to the right side?"

To his surprise, she emerged from the kitchen showcasing her quick change, "I already did."

It was the type of quick wardrobe transformation that Wonder Woman and Clark Kent would have been impressed by.

What's interesting about Frank and Diane's story, is that the same thing happens to people with retirement. They learn after years of parading around in their careers that they left something hanging out. It could be a relationship, passion, hobby, or one's health.

Similar to how Diane felt about her tag, it's not always easy to come to terms and accept it, but rest assured, if some parts of your retirement plan are inside out, it's never too late to turn it around. It starts by peeling off the old and outdated ideas, and answering some personal questions about your retirement plans.

Reflections:

What part of your retirement plan feels inside out?

Is there a situation or area of life that feels like it may be too late to change or turn around?

Write down a time you were surprised by something and you had to do a quick change?

New Adventures

After their parents divorced, Billy, Tom and Patti were required to spend summers with their father who had moved about 45 minutes from their home. With the recent change, they were constantly on the lookout for things to do because they had no friends and few familiar places to go.

One day, their dad told them about a park that was supposedly nearby. He had never been there, but said it contained basketball and tennis courts, swing sets, baseball fields, and even had a small creek.

So he gave them some general direction to its location, and the three set off to find the park. For a few days they cruised around the area on their bikes looking for this park to satisfy their midsummer boredom. After many laps around the same general area and no new clues, they were reminded how hard it is to make your way around a new place or situation. So, they gave up and decided to head in a new direction. Free from the stress of trying to find that which eluded them, their bikes seemed to peddle with greater ease and they all enjoyed the ride much more.

New streets, houses, and cars revealed themselves in a carefree way that solved their monotony and gave them something new to talk about. It wasn't long until they came around a sharp bend, and the elusive park finally came into view. They cheered and raised their hands in victory as they took turns describing parts of the park they were seeing for the first time.

It turned out that the park was located just outside of the general directions they were given. The confines of the map limited the scope of their search, and suppressed those cheerful thoughts and heart-warming feelings that come with a new discovery.

Sometimes we are given ideas, directions, and goals by others, as we pursue them, we hold tightly to what we have been told and where things are supposed to be.

Many times, these instructions can be helpful and necessary to getting started; however, there may be times when we need to let go of what we know and what makes us comfortable. Simply because when we think that the best and only option we have is to hold on, then it's usually the most opportune time to let go.

Reflections:

What is one thing you would like to take in a new direction during retirement?

What would you be giving up or gaining?

What impact might a new location have on you?

Messy Grand Kids

One day a young girl asked her grandmother, "Nana, why do things get so messy all the time?"

She replied, "What do you mean, honey?"

She said, "You know, Nana, when things aren't perfect, like my desk right now. There is stuff is all over the place. It's messy, but just last night I had made it perfect. But it never stays that way."

The grandmother said to her young granddaughter, "Show me what it's like when things are perfect."

She quickly began to move things onto her shelf and into individually assigned containers and said, "There, Nana, now it's perfect. But it won't stay that way."

Now the grandmother asked her, "What happens if I move your pencil box over here to this spot?"

She said, "No, Nana, that's not the right spot, and you're making it messy. It would have to be straight and not crooked the way you put it."

Then she asked her, "What if I moved your markers over here like that?"

"Now you're making it messy again, Nana," she responded.

"What if your drawing pad and this other book are left opened like this?" the grandmother continued.

"That's messy too, Nana!" she replied in a frustrated tone.

The grandmother slowly turned to her granddaughter and said, "Honey, it's not that things get so messy all the time. It's that you have many ways for things to get messy and only *one way* for things to be perfect."

Often times retirement is depicted as this idyllic time filled with long walks on the beach, watching your grandchildren, and worldwide travel, yet it can be anything but that.

Whether its family, the stock market, or your mental and physical health, things may get messy in retirement - especially if you're not prepared to deal with everything that can come with retirement.

In other words, retirement plans that are set in stone and expected to go a certain way, can quickly become frustrating and even disheartening if things change and there is no room to be flexible and adapt.

Reflections:

What are some of the things that could make your retirement messy?

Who do you know who had to make a major adjustment in the way they lived their retirement?

What caused change? How did they adapt?

Dropping The Ball

Luke had finally achieved his goal of playing on the high school varsity football team and was excited to play in the big homecoming game. The stands were packed and as they entered the fourth quarter, he was sent back to receive a punt. The coaches considered Luke a sure-handed player with good speed and potential to play at the next level.

However, none of that mattered when the punt slipped through his hands, bounced between his legs, and slowly rolled end-over-end. He was sandwiched by two opposing players running full speed as the other team recovered the ball with the game on the line.

As if the physical pain wasn't enough, you could see the emotional anguish following the play. Luke was now left facing the 25-yard jaunt back to the sidelines. As you might expect, it seemed like a journey of a thousand miles that had nothing but bad news and angry sentiments waiting for him.

If you have ever made a mistake or caved under pressure, you know how it feels. Luke was ashamed, embarrassed and felt like a failure because he had let down himself, his parents, his classmates and even the team. It suddenly didn't matter that he had an interception earlier in the game or that he scored a touchdown the week before. He was quickly and unexpectedly in a deep dark hole that he never planned for.

While no player ever practices running to the sideline with his head hung low in both guilt and shame, retirees can feel the same way when they slip up. Nobody wants to make a bad investment, become a victim of fraud, or lie to their loved ones about overspending or debt levels. However, it's easy to mishandle money, let your health slip, or misuse others' trust in you.

These types of situations regularly come up in people's lives, yet they are more significant because they aren't tied to a game or half-time popularity contest.

The truth is that everyone is facing a challenge or demon(s) in their lives as a result of some sort of fumble. Which is why one of the most important things you need to do whether you're just a few years away from retirement or already in it, is to PLEASE make sure your part of a good team and are surrounded with supportive people.

You see, when Luke was in the midst of his big homecoming fumble, what didn't get mentioned was what happened when he returned to the sidelines. When he got there, nobody yelled, ridiculed, or chastised him. Instead, he was greeted with high fives, slaps on the back, and smacks on the helmet. The conversation immediately switched to "getting it back" and "turning things around" because that's how teams are trained to think and act. Even the coach chimed in, putting his arm around Luke, "Shake it off and remember to look the ball into your hands and secure it before you take off."

It's also the message and reminders that you may need now or sometime in the future. Secure your family, friends and financial professionals. Don't take off before things are right, and when you fumble, have a team to pick you up and help you focus on the future instead of the past.

Reflections:

How do you feel after you make a mistake or fumble?

Who's on your team? Who can you count on to keep encouraging you and help you pick things up?

What do you need to get a better handle on before taking off for retirement?

It's Called An Echo?

A grandfather and grandson were walking down a canyon when the boy suddenly tripped on a rock, fell, and landed face down.

"OUCH" he screamed! And to his immediate surprise, a voice from the hills hollered back, "OUCH!"

Shaken and afraid, the boy shouted, "WHO ARE YOU?" The answer he received was, of course, "WHO ARE YOU?"

A little embarrassed by his fall, and not knowing what else to do, the young boy yelled again at the canyon walls, "BE QUIET!" In return, the hills answered, "BE QUIET." Grandfather distracts him – you're going to be ok

Puzzled, he looked over to his grandfather. Drawing a deep breath, his granddad shouted, "I LOVE YOU!" His voice echoed back, "I LOVE YOU!"

The man shouted again, "YOU ARE AMAZING!" And the voice returned, "YOU ARE AMAZING!" Now his grandson was smiling, but still he didn't quite understand.

"It's called an echo," explained grandpa, "and it acts like life itself. Life answers your questions and

gives you what you give it." If you want more love, seek to
give more love. If you want more happiness, give others happiness.

Like an echo, retirement is only a product of what you ask and give to it. So, if you want things to be better or different during it, start taking different actions today.

Reflections:

What do you hope your life before retirement will echo?

What has life given back to you based on what you have given to it?

What habits and traditions do you hope to echo or pass onto future generations?

Carrying Heavy Loads

Alan is a retired mechanic and despite some arthritis in his hands, he believes he's stronger and more capable than most 50-year olds. As a result, when Maggie comes home from the grocery store, Alan has this inherent need – some sort of deep rooted pride - to carry in everything from the car in one trip.

Mind you, Alan's mother is living with them and Maggie babysits the grandkids two days a week. So, when he opens the trunk of the car, he is greeted by a sea of grocery bags.

With more determination than planning, he begins to slip the bags over each wrist, carefully leaving a hand available to carry a gallon of milk or laundry detergent. As he walks up the stairs, he quickly comes face to face with his grocery delivery nemesis: The door.

Despite having done this hundreds of times, his mind begins to scramble as he steps onto the porch and tries to figure out how he is going to adjust the bags or manipulate his body to swing open and walk through that door with all the stuff still in his hands. When he finally makes his way through the door and reaches the kitchen table, he releases a big sigh of relief.

However, as a result of trying to do it all at once, something or someone usually suffers - as we all know too well. It could be the loaf of bread that gets squished, the bag of chips that falls out, or the hamburger juice that drips onto the floor. Then there's the throbbing pain in his hand and wrists from trying to carry so much.

Furthermore, there are no real rewards for the expeditious work. Nobody showers him with more love or gratitude for completing the one-trip wonder.

It makes you stop and consider: Why doesn't he just set the bags down or make a couple trips? Right?

The fact is, something very similar can happen on the way to retirement. We're often tasked with carrying and juggling a lot as we approach retirement, but you'll never get through the door with it all. You pour yourself into work, make sacrifices, save and invest regularly and suddenly find yourself on the doorstep, wondering what you may have to adjust or manipulate to walk through the door.

Although many of the things you have when you reach the door are essential for retirement, trying to get everything *through* the door usually means something has suffered along the way. It could be a relationship, healthy lifestyle, desire to experience certain activities, or even the ability to find joy outside of work.

Which aspects of retirement cause you to feel overloaded or burdened?

Since you can't carry it all, what can you set down and come back to later?

What aspects of your life have fallen by the wayside or need to be cleaned-up?

Melting Away

One morning a volunteer named Ron showed up for his shift carrying his favorite lunch, leftover stew. No one knew for sure what was in it, but he was excited beyond description about it. When lunchtime finally arrived, Ron took his prized stew to the microwave like he was carrying a new born baby or piece of priceless art.

Having turned a plastic butter tub into his personal Tupperware for the day, Ron carefully put his container of stew into the microwave, pressed start, and began to whistle and tap his toes like he didn't have a care in the world.

Three minutes later he opened the container lid, expecting to inhale the sweet scent of homemade stew. That's when thing went awry. There was a loud thud that echoed throughout the lunch room. Ron had suddenly chucked his precious lunch into the garbage and was walking away, visibly upset.

"What are you doing?" asked a co-worker.

Sadly, shaking his head, Ron said, "I grabbed the wrong container this morning and just microwaved an entire tub of butter."

The entire room erupted in laughter, and for his next several shifts other volunteers and staff called him "butterfingers."

It's a classic story that makes me laugh at every time I read it, and it also illustrates an important lesson for new and soon-to-be retirees.

Obviously, Ron could have avoided the disappointment by simply checking to see what was in that container a number of different times. He could have checked his precious stew when he grabbed it out of the refrigerator, when he arrived at work, and even before he put it into the microwave.

However, his assumption that he had the right container and it held all the right ingredients, blinded him to the reality of the situation - until it was too late, and lunchtime ended his great expectations.

Reflections:

What precious aspects of your retirement plan are you most confident in?

Think about a time you made a mistake similar to Ron's. What was it, and what signs did you miss along the way?

What's funny about it now?

Overcoming Setbacks

One hot summer day a group of grasshoppers approached a dairy farm. They were in need of an afternoon break and agreed to rest on one of the farm's many large barrels. As they reached the base of the barrel, several of the grasshoppers leaped to the top, hoping to join the rest of their group. To their surprise, there was no lid and they quickly found themselves swimming for their lives in a tub full of milk.

A variety of other insects quickly gathered around the edge of the barrel, laughing, taunting and mocking their inevitable demise. The grasshoppers in the barrel feverishly jumped up and down in an attempt to escape, but their efforts seemed useless. The other insects took joy in mocking their every effort to get out.

One by one, they began to die, except for one grasshopper he seemed to rebuff the scoffs and negative remarks.

The last grasshopper actually seemed to be jumping up and down faster and faster with every taut and jeer. This caused the other insects to laugh and tease louder and more persistently.

Then, by way of a small miracle, the contents of the barrel began to harden. The last grasshopper made such a stir that he actually churned the milk into butter, making it possible for him to jump out.

When he reached the top, the other insects were amazed by his feat. They raised him above their heads and proclaimed him a hero.

What the other insects did not know about their newfound hero was that upon his landing in the creamy milk, his ears were filled with the very substance that saved his life. You see, the milk filled his ears and he could not hear what the other insects were saying to him.

Therefore, when he would look up, he actually thought they were cheering and rooting for him. He used their taunts and jeers to his advantage. When others perceived an inevitable end, he saw a unique opportunity to show his strength to the watching crowd. It was this unique perspective that saved his life!

At different points of life in retirement, you may feel like you've fallen into a barrel full of milk, barely keeping your head above the surface. While people may not be taunting or jeering at you, it can feel like a myriad of things are pulling you down. So, it's crucial to change your perspective and realize your full potential. You've been given these circumstances, resources, and opportunities because you can handle them. With a little time and consistent effort, you'll come out on top - just like other times.

What aspects of your life and retirement feel like they might be pulling you down?

Share a time when you struggled to keep your head above water. How did you survive that time?

Who would you consider a retirement hero - someone who overcame a tough situation, including the jeers and taunts from others?

Staying Young

A local financial advisor was waiting for his appointment to arrive when he saw Dr. Lem pull into the parking lot. He decided to meet him at the door and stuck out his hand to greet him.

To his surprise, Dr. Lem raised his hand, "Sorry, can't do it."

Being curious, the advisor asked, "Are you sick. Is everything okay?'

"I don't want to get you all dirty." Dr. Lem said, "I met some friends this morning for a bike ride and was doing a little maintenance until I realized what time it was, and I just jumped in the car so I wouldn't be late."

"You make it sound like you're gearing up for a big race, or that you're still hitting the road five days a week," chimed his advisor.

"I didn't retire to sit around," remarked Dr. Lem. "I still bike every day of the week at 5:30 a.m. with some friends from the Chamber and Rotary Club. It's a habit I don't want to break. Even though I can't go as fast or far as I used to, it makes me feel alive and well."

"Glad you're taking advantage of your early retirement and making the most of it," observed his advisor. "When I was reviewing your file this morning," he continued, "I noticed you have a birthday coming up soon. Will you be 63 or 64?"

Dr. Lem grinned, "Thanks for the compliment, but I'll be 67." He added, "Mentally I still think I'm 35 or 40 but when I try to get off the floor after playing with the grandkids, my body makes these pops and cracks that say I'm 67, so I'm doing what I can to maximize all the things I can still do."

The conversation between Dr. Lem and his advisor is important for two reasons. First, it highlights the contagious nature of a positive attitude in retirement. When you hear someone use terms like, "It makes me feel alive," it's easy to feel inspired and ready to take on a new challenge.

Second, Dr. Lem recognizes that retirement doesn't automatically come with as much time as you might like, so you could do whatever you want when you want. Situations can change quickly, and you may find yourself less mentally or physically capable, making it essential to continue to do what you can to make the most of your current abilities.

As a result, one could say that Dr. Lem's wealth extends beyond his portfolio because he understands that retirement's most precious assets are a combination of time as well as mental and physical well-being.

What makes you feel alive? When was the last time you truly felt alive?

How are you maximizing all the things you can still do?

How can you use the time you have in retirement to inspire and challenge others?

Blue Collar Wisdom

Bernie was a blue-collar guy who spent his entire life in the manufacturing business. He was not college educated and after many trials and tribulations, he was finally ready to retire and sell his small, auto supplier business.

It was a hefty pay day for a guy who preferred to walk around in his blue uniform with dirty hands. What's interesting is that he wasn't excited about the money or walking away from a business he had poured his life into. Instead, he was glad to be leaving the industry because he was sick of meeting with new company vice presidents and engineers who showed up on the shop floor and didn't know how to read a blueprint. He regularly complained, "They have no clue how the manufacturing process really works."

Time and time again, new engineers and so-called company big shots would show up with their perfect drawings and precise calculations, but within five minutes Bernie could spot several problems. So, he would tell them, "If you machine the part that way, it's going to leave a burr on the edge. Then you'll have to remove the burr in a separate process, or you won't get the seal you need."

Despite his knowledge and years of work experience, they looked at him like he had no idea what he was talking about. This left him feeling frustrated and wondering why he even tried to speak up and help them out.

Unbeknownst to most people, burrs are minuscule pieces of unwanted material that are generally beyond the scope of the naked eye. Surprisingly, they can't be completely eliminated from the manufacturing process, simply because a tool can't enter or exit the machining process without leaving a mark.

There's a definite parallel between this blue-collar manufacturing wisdom and the retirement planning process. Many people start out with a fancy blueprint and a series of precise calculations that they expect will get them to retirement, but along the way, burrs pop up and need to be smoothed out in a separate process. After all, retirement could be considered one of life's biggest modification processes and, as you might imagine, it's pretty common for a few raised edges to remain after someone leaves the work place.

Retirement is like other life events that modify or change us. It doesn't automatically dissolve unwanted or leftover parts. In other words, retiring from your job or career won't necessarily make you feel happy, closer to your spouse, more motivated to take care of your health or slow down your drinking or use of pain meds. In fact, more time and fewer distractions, which tend to come with retirement, might actually make them worse.

Just as burrs can cause manufacturing problems by concentrating stress and increasing the risks of corrosion and unwanted friction, proper retirement planning needs more quality control measures to make sure unwanted things don't complicate everyday retirement life.

Sadly, as most people plan for retirement they spend the majority of their time and energy machining just one single component of a successful transition into retirement - the financial elements. To make matters worse, most of the problems people have in retirement don't have anything to do with money. They fail because there is a breakdown in one or more of other key aspects of retirement, such as the mental, social, physical, or spiritual aspects.

Retirement burrs can come in the form of a sudden or forced retirement, aging parents, adult children, loss of a loved one, divorce, medical diagnosis, a deteriorating social network, natural aging, depression, addiction, financial loss, or some form of fraud to name a few. The recurring list of potential problems constantly threatening retirees demands that they be treated as facts of life in the retirement planning process.

Manufacturing a successful retirement requires new, existing, and future retirees to focus on each and every part instead of assuming one or two components are enough to drive the entire machine. A fancy blueprint or precise calculations just aren't enough. People need a comprehensive process to make sure all the parts of retirement - including the mental, social, physical, and spiritual - mesh perfectly with the financial aspects. Doing so can greatly increases the quality and functionality of life in retirement.

Reflections:

What raised edges or burrs are most likely to slow down your transition into retirement?

What kind of planning have you done beyond your financial blue print that focuses on the everyday life aspects of retirement?

What warnings from other people have you been overlooking or thinking they will work themselves out?

When Things Pile Up

Jerry grew up in the city with a big family that included four brothers and three dogs. He has fond memories of that time except for the fact that they had a small backyard. The combination of three dogs, a tiny yard, and harsh winters meant every spring thaw Jerry and his older brother faced a daunting task. Cleaning up all the dog piles.

Walking out the back door, they were greeted with a sea of dog mess. There wasn't a single blade of grass that remained clean. It was everywhere, and it left the siblings wondering why their parents didn't just tear out the lawn and start over each year.

The pure size and smell of the task seemed pointless. Instead of facing it head on, the boys used their negative thoughts and feelings to start the task by arguing. They argued over who would hold the shovel and who would be the scooper. They disagreed on where to start and how to best accomplish the apparently endless task.

As a result, they wasted a lot of time and energy on things that didn't matter. However, once they got going, and focused on doing the work instead of squabbling, things changed.

As they made progress, negative thoughts about running away to a new family or training the dogs to go to the bathroom in the neighbor's yard disappeared. Together, they worked through it, and the more work they accomplished, the better they felt about being able to escape the confines of the dog piles.

Truth be told, things can pile up on people just before they enter retirement. It can feel not only daunting and pointless, but it can also really start to stink.

People begin to worry about everything: When to take Social Security, the timing of withdrawals, health care costs, a stock market crash, and more. As a result, their retirement date becomes a moving target. It can feel like it will never happen, or that they will never be done working and saving.

That's why it's important for people to understand when it's time to stop over-thinking the situation. You can wonder all day about whether you're scooping or not, when and where to start, or how best to do it. But frankly, you just need to start moving forward, focusing on something positive.

Nobody ever has all of retirement completely figured out, and most of the time when things don't go according to our plans, there is a good lesson to be learned from it. Therefore, when things pile up on you in retirement, be prepared to take on the challenge with the mindset that those piles are only temporary and serve as a gateway to better days and times.

Reflections:

What thoughts and feelings are piling up on you about retirement?

What negative thoughts have you attached to the tasks of planning for retirement?

What is one thing you're ready to stop talking about and start doing?

A Mermaid Surprise

Bill and Marcy had just finished "toddler proofing" their house when their niece was dropped off for the evening. They had some old movies from when their kids were younger and decided to sit down with her and watch the "Little Mermaid" together.

While they had seen the movie several times before, this time was different for Bill because he was struck by a powerful message about his retirement which was just a few years away.

As you may recall, Ariel, the little mermaid, falls in love with a handsome captain and decides to give up her beautiful voice for a pair of legs.

It's a seemingly innocent fable that appears touching and sweet as she is willing to give up a piece of herself for the love of another and a desire to belong.

The problem is that when we are asked to give up our voice or other gifts, we silence what makes us unique and special. We barter who we truly are for what others want or expect us to be.

Another harsh reality is found in Ariel's desire to be loved. No matter how badly we want to love or be loved, if we alter our basic nature to try and accomplish it, a void is created and makes it difficult to survive inside - where it counts the most.

For we are born with only one obligation: To be ourselves, not what others want.

Along the way to retirement, we're taught to be mobile and that it's important to move on and move up. We're taught that our success depends on following along with what others think and believe is the best route to retirement.

But then, many get there and find that the beautiful voice or the special gift they gave up long ago is what they desire to have the most.

Reflections:

What have you traded off during your journey towards retirement?

How has your love for people, places, and things re-directed your road to retirement?

How has your love for yourself and special gifts been impacted? Is there anything missing from you?

Bucket Fillers

An advisor stood before a group of seminar attendees with some items in front of him. He began by quietly picking up a very large, empty jar and proceeded to fill it with golf balls. He then asked the group if the jar was full. They agreed that it was.

The advisor then picked up a box of pebbles and poured them into the jar. He shook the jar lightly. The pebbles rolled into the open areas between the golf balls. Again, he asked if the jar was full. They agreed that it was.

Next, the advisor picked up a box of sand and poured it into the jar. Of course, the sand filled the empty spaces. He asked once more if the jar was full. The attendees responded with a unanimous "yes."

So the advisor produced two cups of coffee from under the table and poured the entire contents into the jar and filled the empty space between the grains of sand. The members laughed.

"Now," said the advisor as the laughter subsided, "I want you to recognize that this jar represents your life. The golf balls are the important things - your family, your children, your health, and your friends. If everything else was lost and only they remained, your life would still be full.

The pebbles are the other things that matter like your job, your house, and your car. The sand is everything else - the small stuff."

"If you put the sand into the jar first," he continued, "there is no room for the pebbles or the golf balls. The same goes for life. If you spend all your time and energy on the small stuff you will never have room for the things that are truly important to you."

"Focus on the things that are critical to your happiness. Play with your children and grandchildren. Take time to get medical checkups. Take your spouse out to dinner, support charities, and others - because the rest is just sand."

A gentleman in the back row raised his hand and asked, "What does the coffee represent?" The advisor smiled and replied, "I'm glad you asked. It just goes to show that no matter how full your life may seem, there's always room for a couple of cups of coffee with a friend."

Reflections:

What do you hope to fill your life with in retirement? What things represent the golf balls, pebbles, and grains of sand?

Who haven't you talked to in a while that you should meet right away for coffee?

What lesson do you hope your life teaches others around you?

Untold Tales

Their first stop for the day was about 20 minutes away. This was the second-time Harold and Lou were paired up as part of a local program that picked up and delivered used furniture to families in need.

Harold was retired and knocking on the door of age 70, but was one of those new-age retirees who isn't frail or incapable. Truthfully, in spite of his age and beer belly, he's one of those guys you wouldn't want to faceoff with in a dark alley. Some people are just born tough as a tank. Despite his hard exterior, Harold is easy to talk to and quick to share a joke or smile.

As they drove along, Lou, who's still a few years away from retirement asked, "How do you like retirement?"

Harold was quick to share "Everything is great. Wish I had done it sooner."

Lou replied in his typical glass-half-empty style, "I hear a lot of people saying that. But I can't believe everything is great and easy just because you don't have to go to work anymore. My dad retired young and seemed miserable most of the time."

There was a long pause and the hum of the highway filled the car. Harold wiggled around, trying to get more comfortable in the driver's seat.

Eventually, he turned to Lou and dropped a retirement bomb that left Lou shell-shocked. It was something Lou had never heard or even thought was possible.

"You know," Harold said, "There's one thing about retirement I can't really put my finger on. It's that I feel bad and guilty about getting a check that I didn't really earn."

Lou's entire body snapped toward him and blurted out that famous line from the 1980's TV show *Different Strokes*, "What choo talkin' 'bout, Willis?"

Lou just couldn't comprehend Harold's dilemma. He wondered how in the heck could someone drive themselves to the same job at the same place for 40 years, work hard, never take all his vacations or allotted sick days, and then feel guilty each time his monthly pension check arrives?

What's interesting about Harold's situation is that he's not alone. Many people are on the verge of the retirement and despite the fact that they did everything they were supposed to do, retirement can feel funny. Ironically, it's not just the tough guys with a rough exterior who are dealing with it. Retirees of different shapes, sizes, and genders express some of the same or similar feelings and don't know what to do about it.

Fortunately for Harold, he found a safe person to have a real conversation about what was going on for him. Although not everyone will deal with this particular feeling, it's important to understand that there may not be a quick fix. But that's okay because the healing process begins by letting it out instead of keeping it in.

That's one reason why I compare the concept of retirement to a massive iceberg, because much of what really goes on in people's hearts and minds during retirement lies below the surface, out of mainstream discussion. But it doesn't have to be that way.

Reflections:

What role does money play in your work life? How might that change in retirement?

What feels funny, strange or awkward about retirement?

What thoughts or feelings have you had that might go against conventional beliefs about retirement?

Looking Behind The Door

"He'll be dead in three to five years," responded Jim to the news that a family friend recently retired.

Jim's wife exclaimed, "James Allen Smith, why would you say such a thing?"

Jim wasn't trying to be disrespectful or say it in a wagering type way, but based on his own experience with life in retirement, he knew something his wife didn't. That the doorway to retirement is just as likely to be an end as it is a beginning.

In this case, Jim's friend Al was a life-long auto worker. In fact, the last 45 years of his life was devoted to one company. He had worked at the same building and with the same people for his entire life.

His old-school ways and beliefs were the proverbial nail in the coffin. After all, he had only reached this stage in life through sheer hard work, determination, and regular sacrifice. But he hadn't applied any of those qualities to preparing for everyday life in retirement.

Outside of work, he had fractured relationships with his kids, he wasn't in great shape, and his passion seemed to be complaining about current political events. As a result, retirement was a closing door and as Jim predicted, Al passed away four years into retirement due to health complications and a divorce.

A door is the perfect illustration for retirement because it can imply both positive and negative things. It can provide an aspect of safety when you chain and lock the door.

It can be a surprise and mystery since no one knows what goes on behind closed doors. Or, it can be a form of rejection when someone closes the door on you. Yet, it can even offer limitless possibilities when a new door opens up.

Therefore, in order to make sure it swings wide open and you don't end up like Al, understand that a successful career doesn't always translate into a successful retirement. It's important to recognize that most of the stuff that made your career a big success won't automatically translate into a happy retirement home life.

In Al's case, the hard-nosed, self-centered approach that helped him get through a 45-year career as a manager and compile ample savings didn't get him far in retirement.

Unfortunately, when retirement doesn't go as planned, it's common to turn to your old trusty work tools to fix it. But in retirement things can rust quickly and cause more damage than you might expect.

Furthermore, being open-minded to the new ways to manage your life in retirement, ends up working for you like adding oil to a rusty hinge. A flexible mindset, will help you smooth things out and reduce annoying, unnecessary noise. Then with regular attention and maintenance, you can acquire and use new tools to keep the door open and functioning.

Reflections:

What makes you successful at work and in your field? What's similar and different to what makes successful at home and in relationships?

What aspects of retirement make you feel safe? Which ones do you expect to surprise you?

What do you think goes on behind closed doors in retirement? What doors are you most excited to open?

I'll Take The $20

A speaker began his workshop by holding up a $20 bill, asking the group, "Who would like this twenty dollars?"

As audience members raised their hands, he said, "I am going to give this money to one of you," but then he crumpled up the bill. "Who still wants it," he asked? All the hands remained in the air.

"Well," he continued, "what if I do this?" He dropped it on the ground and started to grind it into the floor with his shoe. He picked up the crumpled and dirty bill - and asked again, "Anyone still want it?" All hands went back into the air.

"My friends, this simple demonstration offers new and soon-to-be retirees a very valuable lesson," he said. "No matter what I did to the money, you still wanted it because it did not decrease in value. It was never worth less than $20."

"In retirement, losing the career identity you spent a lifetime creating, and facing new and unknown circumstances, can make you feel crumpled or ground into the dirt. But work is what you do, not who you are. No matter much or how little money you have saved for retirement, it doesn't affect your true value."

Dirty or clean, crumpled or finely creased, you are always priceless, especially to those who love you.

The worth of our lives comes not from what we do or what we have, but in *who we are.*

Count your blessings, not your problems. And don't be afraid to make this phase of your life your most memorable.

Too many people today confuse who they are with what they do. They feel valuable based on what they have accumulated. However, neither possessions nor accomplishments can love you back.

Reflections:

Who are you when you are not at work?

What aspects of work are going to be the most difficult for you to replace?

What people and things can provide that greatest return on the love you offer or direct towards them?

Banker Versus Fisherman

A Wall Street banker was taking a much-needed vacation in a small coastal village when a small boat with just one fisherman docked. The boat had several large, fresh fish in it. The banker was impressed by the quality of the fish and asked the fisherman, "How long did it take for you to catch them?"

He replied, "Only a little while."

The banker then asked, "Why didn't you stay out there longer and catch more fish?

The fisherman replied, "With this I have more than enough to meet my family's needs."

The banker responded sharply, "But what do you do with the rest of your time?"

The fisherman replied, "I sleep in, fish a little, play with my children, take a nap with my wife, stroll into the village each evening where I sip wine and play guitar with some friends"

The Wall Street banker sensing an opportunity suggested, "I could help you become wealthy and build the life people dream of. We could start by having you fish for a few more hours each day. Then we would sell the fish and use the proceeds to buy you a bigger boat."

Proud of his own sharp thinking, he elaborated on a grand scheme which could bring even bigger profits, "With the additional income from the larger boat, you could buy several other boats until you eventually had an entire fleet of fishing boats. At that point you could stop selling your catch to the middleman and go directly to the processor, eventually opening your own cannery. You could leave this tiny coastal village and move to Los Angeles or New York City to expand your enterprise and control the product, processing and distribution."

The fisherman asked, "How long will all of this take?"

After a rapid mental calculation, the banker said, "Probably 15-20 years, maybe less if you work really hard."

"But what happens then?" asked the curious fisherman

The banker laughed and remarked, "That's the best part. When the time is right you would take your company public, sell your company stock and become very rich. You could make millions."

"Millions? Really? What would I do with all that?" asked the *wise* fisherman.

The business banker boasted, "Then you would

retire. You could move to a small coastal fishing village where you would sleep late, fish a little, play with your grandkids, take a nap with your wife, and stroll to the village in the evenings where you could sip wine and play your guitar with your friends."

This is a powerful parable that brings into question the paths we take and the outcomes people desire in retirement. Can it be as simple as finding satisfaction with who you are and what you do? Or, does it have to be a long and arduous journey to better appreciate the things we have? Will you end up somewhere or someone that you already are? That is the question.

Reflections:

What are you fishing for in retirement? What do you need to feel happy and fulfilled?

What are you sacrificing today that you may not be able to get back in retirement?

Which aspects of your current life to you want to maintain in retirement?

Encore Summary

As you can tell from this book, I love telling stories to help illustrate my beliefs and philosophy. To put an exclamation point of this body of work, I've saved one of my favorites for last.

A retired grandfather was watching his grandchildren while his daughter was at work. He was struggling to find the motivation and patience to make the most of his time with them. His task was complicated by one grandson who was constantly bored and couldn't stay focused on a single task.

Grandpa tried several activities to occupy this little one, but nothing worked, and he was getting frustrated. Finally, he picked up a magazine, flipped through it, and stopped at a brightly colored picture of the Earth.

He pulled the page out, ripped the picture into bits, and scattered them on the floor. "If you can put this puzzle back together, I'll give you a dollar," he told the ~~busy~~ boy.

This, he assumed, would occupy the kid for some time.

Not ten minutes later, his grandson walked up to him, smiling ear-to-ear, with the puzzle completed. The grandfather was impressed to see that he had finished so quickly, and that all the pieces were neatly arranged and the picture of the world was back in order. "How did you finish so quickly?" he asked.

The proud young man replied, "Easy! There was a picture of a person on the other side of the world. I just put a piece of paper on the floor, put the picture of the person back together, and then flipped it over. I figured if I got the person right, the world would be right, too!"

Grandpa laughed, handed his grandson a dollar, and thanked him for the valuable life lesson: "If the person is right, the world will be right, too."

I firmly believe that when individuals or couples have their personal retirement plans on track, it's much easier to address the financial issues. Walt Disney once said, "When your values are clear, your decisions are easy." A meaningful statement that suggests it's easier to create a more meaningful retirement by focusing on you and what's most important to you rather than the dollars and cents of it all.

Thank you for joining me on this journey and for the opportunity to explore retirement's edges together. I hope your thoughts and plans about retirement have been dramatically transformed and that the work you've done helps you blaze new trails for yourself, your family, and others.

Certified Professional Retirement Coach Certification (CPRC)

Now more than ever, advisors must realize that there is more to retirement that just the dollars and cents. Fact is, people are failing at retirement at an alarming rate because they aren't prepared for the non-financial aspects of it. Use our certification to:

- Protect and grow your business by making deeper, more emotional connections with clients

- Use non-financial topics and conversations to generate new business like never before

- Gain a competitive advantage that will magnify your influence and establish you as a go-to expert

- Find new value in your role by coaching clients on retirement topics that they want and need, but don't know who to turn to

- Be more referable because of the impact you are having on others

The Certified Professional Retirement Coach™ designation is an accepted CE provider for CFP®, IMCA, ICF, SHRM and is listed at FINRA.org

1st module is **Free** at CertifiedRetirementCoach.org

Plus Save $500 with coupon code **CPRCSAVE**

Inspire, Educate, & Engage With Retirement Rx

Make Retirement Rx available to clients, employees, and organization members as the ideal way to help them start talking about and planning for the non-financial aspects of retirement.

Bulk orders save money as well as build trust and confidence.

Physical copies of the book send a clear message that you are concerned and interested in helping people make a successful transition from work-life to home life…. And that retirement isn't just about the dollars and cents.

Retirement Rx
- Differentiates you and your organization
- Says that you care about them
- Positions you as a wellness advocate
- Offers real life ideas and applications
- Helps make an impact in others lives
- Enhances your professional legacy

Bulk pricing starts at just $8 per book for as little as 25 copies. Orders can be completed online at RetirementProject.org or by calling 888-267-1138.

About The Author: Robert Laura

 Robert Laura is the Retirement Activist who is committed to changing the way people think about and prepare for every aspect of retirement. His nationally syndicated columns at Forbes.com and Financial Advisor Magazine reflect his ground-breaking efforts to challenge the status quo of traditional planning.

As a former social worker and certified personal trainer turned money manager, author, and retirement coach he has found that retirement is among the most fascinating, yet least understood, phases of life.

Robert founded RetirementProject.org and the Certified Professional Retirement Coach designation. He has also authored several books including *Retirement Rx* and *Naked Retirement*.

In addition to his own writings, he frequently appears in major business media and has been speaking and teaching economic, investment, and coach training programs for over 15 years.

He is married to his amazing wife Amie, and together they have a blended family with four children: Connor, Ava, Lucas, and Drake.

You can learn more at <u>RetirementProject.org</u>